The
Prophetic
PACE

Lessons for Millennial Prophets

CEDRIC WRIGHT II

Lynetta's Pen Publishing
Denver, Colorado

Lynette's Pen Publishing
Aurora, CO 80014
The Prophetic Pace: Lessons for Millennial Prophets Cedric Wright —1st ed.
ISBN 9781729786659

Table of Contents

Introduction

After I finished my last mini book, I said to myself I'd never write another book. I felt like that book was horrible even though I sold over 6000 copies.

But I saw the temple and market place prophets suffering under the siege of tradition, religion and ignorance.

Once you grab these lessons you will not only be able to escape the wiles of the enemy but to conquer the things which are keeping you from being successful within the prophetic.

These lessons are in no particular order but they are important lessons to know. Being an authentic prophet is no easy task, especially a millennial prophet.

It's in Jesus' name that I pray that this book will revive you and encourage you to prophesy again and to continue to run at the pace of a prophet!

@ProphetCedric

1] We Fight a Real Devil

One of the worst feelings in the world is to have something stolen from you. Many questions come to mind. Did I attract this to myself? Did I not protect my things? Did I allow people into my space that I should not have?

The truth may be many of those things or others not mentioned. One truth is certain. There was a breech in security somewhere, or perhaps there was no security at all!

Sadly, many Christians today do not realize that we have an enemy; the devil. Some groups even suggest that the devil isn't real but rather a moral tool or a scare tactic to keep us from sinning and behaving poorly.

The devil is real and is responsible for demonic activity. He is a demonic king and is responsible for an entire demonic kingdom and system.

DEMONIC ACTIVITY IN THE EARTH

There are demonic princes, princesses, officials, principalities, powers, authorities, international, national and regional representatives, demonic agendas, plans, plots, churches, pastors, witches and warlocks.

There are demonic intelligence agents who spy and watch the saints and work in collaboration with time sensitive cures to devour the saints.

There are demonic strengths which give demons and body vessels or demonically possessed individuals the power to complete their diabolical assignments.

There are demonic inventors. These spirits use wicked imagination to create tools, products or merchandise to further a demonic ecosystem.

There are demonic teachers; spirits which train and teach of old ancient spells and rituals.

The demonic kingdom is real and very organized. There is an agenda that they are after.

These are spirits who don't need sleep. Their energy is fueled by the devil. The only reason this kingdom knows how to operate is because it patterns itself after the Kingdom of Heaven in which God is the King.

Both angels and demons are categorized into 3 different rankings and 3 different sub-rankings within each classification. There is 9 different classifications altogether (Marvelous History by Sebastien Michaelis). The angelic rankings will be listed later in the book.

The list below is of demonic princes which were once angels that were Seraphim, Cherubim and Thrones before the great fall

First hierarchy

- *Beelzebub* was a prince of the Seraphim, just below Lucifer. Beelzebub, along with Lucifer and Leviathan, were the first three angels to fall. He tempts men with pride.
- *Leviathan* was also a prince of the Seraphim who tempts people to give into heresy.
- *Asmodeus* was also a prince of the Seraphim, burning with desire to tempt men into wantonness.
- *Berith* was a prince of the Cherubim. He tempts men to commit homicide, and to be quarrelsome, contentious, and blasphemous.
- *Astaroth* was a prince of Thrones, who tempts men to be lazy.
- *Verrine* was also prince of Thrones, just below Astaroth. He tempts men with impatience.
- *Gressil* was the third prince of Thrones, who tempts men with impurity.
- *Sonneillon* was the fourth prince of Thrones, who tempts men to hate.

Second hierarchy

The second hierarchy includes Powers, Dominions, and Virtues.

- Carreau was a prince of Powers. He tempts men with hardness of heart.
- Carnivale was also a prince of Powers. He tempts men to obscenity and shamelessness.
- Rosier was the second in the order of Dominions. He tempts men to sexual impurity.
- Belias was the prince of Virtues. He tempts men with arrogance and women to be vain, raise their children as wantons, and gossip during mass.

Third hierarchy

The third hierarchy includes Principalities, Archangels, and Angels.

- Olivier was the prince of the Archangels. He tempts men with cruelty and mercilessness toward the poor.
- Luvart was prince of Angels. At the time of Michaelis's writing, Luvart was believed to be in the body of Sister Madeleine.
- Verrier was the prince of Principalities. He tempts men against the vow of obedience.

THE DEVIL'S FUNCTION IN THE EARTH

The devil is an imitator and liar, and is well informed. After all, he's been here since time has started. He understands patterns and the behavior patterns of God. If he can get us to separate from the divine pattern, he can successfully derail us from our divine agenda. That's his ultimate goal.

Some of our problems on earth didn't come from earth. This is not to scare you or have you afraid of the devil, but he's like fire. It can be dangerous if you are not careful and you don't understand the "rules" of the fire.

The devil and his demonic agents still have a function that is necessary. We cannot afford to overlook the scripture *"All things work together..." (Romans 8:28)*

God had a meeting with His sons regarding the world. During the meeting Satan also came. How did he know that God and the sons were having a meeting? Was he invited? Either way, Satan was present when God had to get an update on his whereabouts; his assignment.

God began to take attendance. When He got to Satan, He asked the question, "Where are you coming from?"

Satan replied, "I have been everywhere all over the earth."

Since God knows all things and there is nothing outside of his authority, He didn't bother to ask why he was roaming, because that was obviously his current assignment. God jumped right to it and said, "Well, have you considered Job?"

God suggested for Job to be tried because God gave Satan the assignment to show him that there is a creature that *loves me for me*. Note if there's nothing outside of his authority, it means everyone must have been assigned to do a certain thing by God Himself.

Many Christians ignorantly think that they have a right to rebuke the devil on their own. They don't know that the devil is only doing his job; what he has been assigned to do since his fall from grace!

I personally don't accredit all havoc and turmoil to the devil. Mortal men can cause great damage without the assistance of the devil or a demonic entity.

KINGDOMS ARE DIVINELY ORGANIZED

Kingdoms are organized in rank and in order. Your spiritual ranking will determine the type of demonic spirits you will have to confront.

A lot of people want to be apostles I have noticed recently. What they don't understand is that Apostles must confront high ranking demons, the reason why is because Apostles are statesman or ambassadors of the

Kingdom of God. They must deal with demonic and spiritual statesmen. Each office is privy to certain information and a particular authority backed by God Himself. If you are not called to a particular office and you attempt to operate in that office, you put yourself in great danger. You must make your calling and election sure. You need to know where you rank.

Since Satan is the lord and king of the demonic realm, unless you rank as a king like Job, Israel (Jacob), David or the like, you will not confront Satan directly. You may have to confront and battle with lower ranking demons and spirits, but you won't deal directly with him unless you are within his ranking.

Our spiritual ranking in God gives us authority to counteract demonic spirits, while it also gives us the permission to operate as fellow workmen with angels and other spiritual beings. If we attempt to operate outside of our spiritual authority or ranking we open ourselves up to demonic attacks, because we are moving outside of our safe zone or authority.

Unless God has called you to a national level, you have no right or authority to fight against demonic spirits which have strongholds over nations.

People want to go to the nations but don't even have any ranking over the street in their neighborhood!

It is imperative that you know who you are in God. If you fail to investigate and seek God about your spiritual position, role, and ranking, you will open yourself up to great attacks.

THE LEVIATHAN

In the book of Job chapter 41, there is a description of a water beast named "the leviathan". This monster was the natural dispensation of a Satanic prince. Here is a list of questions regarding this beast.

1. Can you catch him with a hook?
2. Can you use a rope?
3. Will he make pleas with you?
4. Will he make covenants with you to make you his servant?
5. Will traders bargain with him?
6. Will they divide him up among merchants?
7. Can you penetrate with a harpoon?

These questions speak of the demonic prince. He is not easy to catch. He's so cunning that most of the time, he will make us think that the reasoning behind certain things is "natural" or "normal". If you think it's supposed to happen you won't oppose it or even regard it as an attack or demonic.

He understands the power of agreements. During the great temptations of Jesus and with the Mother of the garden Eve, the devil attempted to make covenants and agreements with them so that we owe him and he will then have ownership over them.

He can't be reached or penetrated with any natural thing or reasoning because he is a spirit. We must deal with him in the spirit. Therefore, it is very important that we have and use the gifts of the Spirit and that our spiritual armor is full activated.

You must have permission or authorization to rebuke the devil. You cannot rebuke the devil anytime you want. Understand your ranking. There are demons, which are low ranking devils, which we can rebuke. But, do not start spiritual fights without permission or if you are in fellowship with darkness. If you do, you'll make yourself a target for demonic attacks.

This is why we must be seated with Christ in heavenly places because Christ has the power and authority over satan and all of his kingdom. In warfare we must be mindful of the rules and laws of the battlefield. It is unwise to just run into a battle without a plan. You cannot plan an attack without understanding your power and authority. You need to know what you can and cannot do.

We have been conditioned to think that we are singular beings that are a result of time, space and matter. This is only a partial truth; aka a lie. We are a triune being made up of a spirit, soul, and body. Just like God is a triune being, which consist of God the Father, God the Son, and God the Holy Spirit.

We have dual presences now that our spirits have been quickened back to life upon us accepting Jesus as our

Savior. Thus, our roles are both in the spirit and in the natural. If the devil can make you think and agree that you're trapped in the natural realm only, he can steal things from you in the spirit which will then have a natural effect. You will be clueless and a victim.

THE CAUSAL REALM

The spiritual realm is the causal realm. Everything we see is a result of things we cannot see.

I recall reading a facebook post from Apostle Paul Williams that said "The spirit world governs the physical world. Now, let me tell you what this means. What you see happening in your physical world is as a result of what has already happened in the spiritual world. Before anything takes place physically, it has already happened spiritually. Secondly, the state of your spirit man determines the state of your physical man, and the state of your spiritual world determines the state of your physical world."

I was so happy to see this with my own eyes because I knew this was true but I had not heard or seen anyone else say this. I knew by way of the Holy Spirit but did not at the time have proof.

Let's deal with the spirit of a man for a second. It is the spirit of a person that drives him or her to do whatever is that they feel led or want to do. The spirit is the driving force behind us. When God wants to promote you he first promotes your spirit. When the devil wants to attack you he first attacks your spirit. The reason why is because the spiritual realm give way to everything that happens in the natural realm. This is the reason we call it the causal realm.

We have a physical body and we have a spiritual body much like the physical. If your hands are chained in the spirit, there is no way you will prosper in your endeavors. Whatever you touch will quickly come to dust. The reason why, is because the spiritual you must be addressed before the natural you. If you want to change, it must start with your spirit first.

When you lost your first business, more than likely, it was a result of something being stolen from you in the spirit realm.

When our marriages and families are hit, or when divorce suddenly is an option, or our children run away, these are results of something happening in the spirit realm. Because we are ignorant of Satan's devices, we do one of two things if not both:

1) Some of us react carnally. We treat people the way they treat us and let people take us out of our character. This will cause us to surrender our divine authority, which in turn, will allow more hardships to occur. We then begin to work with the enemy. This is because we don't acknowledge our dual roles.

2) Some of us will take matters into our own hands. We will attempt to rebuke the devil and try to tell him what he's not going to win. We'll go on flesh starving days that we think is fasting. If your fast is not the Lord's fast, it's called "starvation".

Then, we start calling people devils. We don't realize that we can, with permission and authority, rebuke a demon and save the man. But we destroy the man, and the devil is still present.

"Yet if he is caught, he must pay sevenfold, though it costs him all the wealth of his house." (Proverbs 6:31 NIV)

The part we get happy about is getting the seven times the amount that was stolen, forgetting or not noticing that this only happens if you can identify the crook. What does he look like?

You must be able to notice him and his ways! You must be familiar with the spirit realm. You must be able to see and hear in the spirit. We must know what the devil looks like, even if he is in others. Failure to know will leave you a victim.

Today, if someone steals from you and is not caught, how can you recover your things? I'm sure you're thinking, "I thought you just said we can't catch the devil with a hook or rope and that we shouldn't."

That is correct. But, we must now move into another paradigm which will allow you to know the only power that can destroy all the powers of the enemy, even leviathan. This is the power of God.

In order to successfully combat and confront the demonic kingdom, you have to do it by the spirit of God. The God in you will give you what you need to conquer and catch the thief.

DISCERNMENT IS KEY

One of the most important gifts that you must have activated in your life is the gift of discernment. Discernment is needed and available to all of us through the Holy Spirit.

What if you could see the face behind the face? What if you could know what you could not know? Think about the advantage you would have if you could see the spirit(s) operating behind the scenes.

The bible informs us that our fight is not against flesh and blood but against spirits. In the past I found myself disappointed in a person instead of realizing that it wasn't them that I was warring against, but demonic spirits.

There is a difference between carnal discernment and spiritual discernment. In order to be successful, you must have spiritual discernment. Carnal discernment is based upon natural knowledge and experiences.

For example, if you've ever been depressed you know the signs and symptoms of depression. You notice the signs because of that experience. Immature Christians tend to rely on their carnal discernment. They are usually badly mistaken.

One time, I was at a rather large church wearing "street wear," which I usually do, especially if I am not ministering. As the minister finished preaching a rather compelling message, one of the members of that congregation walked up to me very sincerely and asked me to walk with her up to the altar of the church and to give my life to Christ.

I told her that I knew God. She then attempted to prophesy out of her flesh and said, "God is going to use you one day to minister and change your life but you first need to be saved. God needs to know you."

I laughed because I knew she was only saying that because of my attire. She thought that because I wasn't dressed under the religious rules in which she was accustomed, that I didn't know Jesus. I thought this thing was rather comical. I am fully secure in my relationship with God.

This type of assumption can cause harm to people. She could have offended me to the point that I wouldn't come back. This also could have made me think that prophecy wasn't real. I told her that her desire to see souls won was amazing but to be careful that she doesn't use her carnal mind or discernment. People could be hurt. I then saw members of the church tell her who I was. She looked so ashamed. I hope she learned her lesson, but if not I learned mine.

Spiritual discernment is a knowing and seeing signs of things which are not noticed in the natural realm. It will allow you to know what spirits are causing behaviors in people and behaviors in our own lives.

For example, when I was a young prophet I was introduced to a lady. Everyone was impressed by her knowledge of the bible and her ability to function in the supernatural.

The Holy Spirit told me that He was going to teach me something and to set up a meeting up with her. On the appointed day and time of the meeting, I brought a friend with me because I was very scared, I knew God was up to something. We met with the lady, and while we were talking the Holy Spirit informed me that she was a witch, and that I was her assignment. Childishly, I tried to argue back and forth with the Holy Spirit and said "But look at her, she doesn't look like a witch. She uses bible verses. She is friendly to the poor and needy. She even ministers to people. Some people in the community tithe to her!"

The Holy Spirit then told me to try the spirit. I did, according to the scripture.

But if someone claims to be a prophet and does not acknowledge the truth about Jesus, that person is not from God. Such a person has the spirit of the Antichrist, which you heard is coming into the world and indeed is already here. 1 John 4:3 (NLT)

I asked her, "Can you say Jesus is Lord?"

She refused and got very angry. She began to demonically declare things. As she did, the Holy Spirit gave me the word of God to counteract the demonic declarations.

While I was combating, I was thinking, how do I know all of these scriptures? How did I know this woman, who appeared to be a woman of God, was a witch and a demonic agent? This is when God activated the gift of discernment in me. Even today, I can spot a witch a mile away. I don't confront every witch, but if the Holy Spirit instructs me, I will without fear.

Discernment places us ahead of demonic attacks and assignments. It gives us a greater advantage. God wants us to be the head and not the tail. Without discernment you can only be reactive to demonic attacks and plans and not proactive.

In order to be successful in spiritual warfare, we must have a system or plan in place before an attack. It does us no good to get security after a robbery. The goal is to be ready for an attack. This is why it is important to concentrate when God speaks. It is not God's will that we be ambushed.

Therefore we must pay much closer attention to what we have heard, lest we drift away from it. For since the message declared by angels proved to be reliable, and every transgression or disobedience received a just retribution, how shall we escape if we neglect such a great salvation? It was declared at first by the Lord, and it was attested to us by those who heard, while God also bore witness by signs and wonders and various miracles and by gifts of the Holy Spirit distributed according to his will. Hebrew 2:1-4 (ESV)

If we don't obey the voice of the Lord, not only about salvation but anything He says, whatever happens to us is our fault. It will be a just action. This is a huge responsibility that we must not take lightly.

If I say to the wicked, 'You shall surely die,' and you give him no warning, nor speak to warn the wicked from his wicked way, in order to save his life, that wicked person shall die ford his iniquity, but his blood I will require at your hand. But if you warn the wicked, and he does not turn from his wickedness, or from his wicked way, he shall die for his iniquity, but you will have delivered your soul. Again, if a righteous person turns from his righteousness and commits injustice, and I lay a stumbling block before him, he shall die. Because you have not warned him, he shall die for his sin, and his righteous deeds that he has done shall not be remembered, but his blood I will require at your hand. But if you warn the righteous person not to sin, and he does not sin, he shall surely live, because he took warning, and you will have delivered your soul." Ezekiel 3:18-21 (NLT)

Hearing from God and being able to discern comes with great responsibilities. This is serious business!

We wrestle not against flesh and blood but against principalities and powers of darkness in high places (Ephesians 6:12). Therefore, without discernment we wouldn't even be able to detect a demonic spirit. We need more than intellect.

And to bring to light for everyone what is the plan of the mystery hidden for ages in God who created all things, so that through the church the manifold wisdom of God might now be made known to the rulers and authorities in the heavenly places. (Ephesians 3:9-10)

Now that we are in Christ, God through His wisdom (we have access through discernment), wants to make known to us the powers that exist, both in the demonic kingdom and in the Divine Kingdom.

Human intellect is limited and is neither valid nor authorized to deal in these realms. But, the wisdom of God overrules and trumps all other knowledge and wisdom. Discernment gives us access to the wisdom of God. The wisdom of God is brilliant.

But where shall wisdom be found? and where is the place of understanding? Man knoweth not the price thereof; neither is it found in the land of the living. The depth saith, It is not in me: and the sea saith, It is not with me. It cannot be gotten for gold, neither shall silver be weighed for the price thereof. It cannot be valued with the gold of Ophir, with the precious onyx, or the sapphire. The gold and the crystal cannot equal it: and the exchange of it shall not be for jewels of fine gold. No mention shall be made of coral, or of pearls: for the price of wisdom is above rubies. The topaz of Ethiopia shall not equal it, neither shall it be valued with pure gold Whence then cometh wisdom? and where is the place of understanding? Seeing it is hid from the eyes of all living, and kept close from the fowls of the air. Destruction and death say, We have heard the fame thereof with our ears. God understandeth the way thereof, and he knoweth the place thereof. For he looketh to the ends of the earth, and seeth under the whole heaven; To make the weight for the winds; and he weigheth the waters by measure. When he made a decree for the rain, and a way for the lightning of the thunder: Then did he see it, and declare it; he prepared it, yea, and searched it out. And unto man he said, Behold, the fear of the Lord, that is wisdom; and to depart from evil is understanding. (Job 28:12-28)

Because you are now able to identify the thief through the gift of discernment and the wisdom of God, you can expect to receive seven times what was stolen from you. That is because you will be able to identify the thief, and through a process of prayer you will receive back the things that were stolen. I encourage you to get into prayer and to ask God to give you the gift of discernment so that you are not open to demonic intruders.

"He gives one person the power to perform miracles, and another the ability to prophesy. He gives someone else the ability to discern whether a message is from the Spirit of God or from another spirit. Still another person is given the ability to speak in unknown languages, while another is given the ability to interpret what is being said." 1 Corinthians 12:10 (NLT)

Do as the bible tells us, and test the spirit to see whether it is of God or not. Not everyone who says they are a prophet is a prophet. They may want a profit. Not everyone who says they are a minister is a minister. Don't be afraid to ask them of whom or by whose authority do they come by.

Dear friends, do not believe everyone who claims to speak by the Spirit. You must test them to see if the spirit they have comes from God. For there are many false prophets in the world. (1 John 4:1 NLT)

We must have the gift of discernment in order to know whether the prophet is speaking correctly or saying things that might be wrong. I call them half-truths, but they don't contain the spirit of truth. Let's look at how the apostles actively used the gift of discernment.

"One day as we were going down to the place of prayer, we met a demon-possessed slave girl. She was a fortune-teller who earned a lot of money for her masters. She followed Paul and the rest of us, shouting, "These men are servants of the Most High God, and they have come to tell you how to be saved." This went on day after day until Paul got so exasperated that he turned and said to the demon within her, "I command you in the name of Jesus Christ to come out of her." And instantly it left her." Acts 16:16-18 NIV

This young lady was a fortune teller. She seemed to be supporting their ministry, telling others that they had a message from God. She was providing free marketing. She seemed pretty normal. If they would have seen the spirit, they would have sought God on how to deal with it then. And no one in their right mind would allow a knowingly demonically possessed person to be a part of their ministry team. She had the right message but from the wrong spirit.

I've dealt with the spirit of Jezebel (2 Kings 9) a few times and one of the questions I would ask God was, *Why didn't I notice.* I didn't notice at first because I didn't use the gift of discernment when I was a young prophet.

For instance, when we read the scripture, Jezebel seemed to be very noticeable with her painted face and actions. I can almost imagine her voice. With carnal discernment I would probably say that she was a loud, mean, controlling woman, who loved the make-up counter at the department stores. That would be wrong.

A spirit can use any type of body open and available for use. (Is the reason and importance of being filled with the Holy Spirit.) She doesn't let you know she is coming to kill you or your ministry. It would be foolish to think that any demonic spirit would present that type of information. If you were aware immediately you would be able to counteract.

Most often Jezebel is seemingly humble, and comes in the garments of a servant. She seems willing to help, trustworthy, kind even. She is very resourceful, having tons of connections. She provides you with security and will beat down in your face any other spirit near you. She will convince you that she is your only support system, that whatever you need she'll handle it. She'll pay the bills in the ministry or at least act like she cares about it. She will, out of supposed love for you, expose the imperfect people who actually do love you. She will work you until you are defending her, working for her. Prophesying for her, she'll get you to a point where you won't make a decision without her, even questioning the things that God has given you directly from the throne room. Now, her opinion matters more than you own.

At this point you will become so insecure that you think everyone is against you and that no one loves you or supports you but her and the Jezebel conspirers. These people are in alliance with her agenda and oftentimes don't even know it. They have different roles. To make you feel accommodated and taken care of. If you felt anything else you would react.

This is why you need discernment active in your life, especially the apostles and prophets. Just as the young woman in Acts 16, her and Jezebel were both very helpful in the natural. Since Jezebel has the person so wrapped up into her system, when you leave the system or attempt to withdraw, you will look foolish in the eyes of men. This is why the prophet Elijah felt he was the only one left. He was the only one able to see behind the painted face.

God raised up a prophet named Jehu who saw past the face present and spoke a word to the Jezebel conspirers. This word, because he was the prophet, called to expose and defeat this spirit, caused a prophetic quake to those who were hypnotized by her aroma and cunning accommodations.

The prophetic, the voice of God asked, "Who's side are you on?"

This question involves other questions:

Why am I doing this?

Is this support or bondage?

Is this the will of the Lord for me?

Who benefits from these things?

Who am I really being loyal to?

Is God getting glory from this?

Is God the true center or is it self-promotional or marketable?

Am I fully relying on the spirit of God, or what the spirit can do?

One question woke up the two eunuchs out of a soul sleep with them realizing that she had cost them their manhood and identity. A eunuch is a man who has been castrated for service. They cannot produce and move into the third dimension of manhood. They can go from boy to man, but never to fatherhood.

The power of that question changed their lives. One of the first things that the spirit of discernment will do is ask you questions and you will also ask questions. Why does this keep happening? It will position you to see past the things which are designed to keep you from looking. It forces you to answer this question prophetically. What are you doing and who are you doing it for?

Those two men grabbed a hold of Jezebel by permission or instruction of the prophetic strategy and threw her down to the ground, and the dogs ate her.

Because Jezebel was unholy and her worship was not considered sacred, she was given over to dogs!

Do not give dogs what is sacred; do not throw your pearls to pigs. If you do, they may trample them under their feet, and turn and tear you to pieces (Matthew 7:6)

If you are in a position that you can't produce in the spirit, you'll never have fruit. Fruit is required. The bible tells us that we would know them by their fruits.

To be spiritually castrated is the result of being in a Jezebelic atmosphere. But this is also to make sure that the demonic system cannot penetrate the divine. There are other effects that castration has beyond the obvious; it can affect your voice so that you can never speak within the lower tones. Spiritually, you will never be able to speak concerning the deep things of God. It will force you to sound like a juvenile. Therefore, you can only deal with juvenile things never the depths of the prophetic.

The Prophetic word; are words, thoughts, and ideas from the mouth of God echoed through the mouth of God's prophets. God's word or presence is never diminished by its changing of vessels. God is no less God in me than He is in the throne room of heaven.

When God speaks, things, places, people, objects, the seen, and unseen are required to fulfill the words in which God had spoken.

Our greatest example is, in the beginning God said in the presence of darkness, let there be light. Darkness can't turn into light, light was somewhere but not activated until God spoke!

The prophetic realm knows what is needed is available and even present but not activated. This is why some of us would never have gotten into ministry until the prophetic word activated that desire.

2] Using Prayer as a Tool

LEVELS, DIMENSIONS, AND REALMS

There are tons of information on the topic of prayer. There are books, tapes, teachings and so much more. However, we still seem to not understand the importance of prayer because there are levels, dimensions, and realms of prayer.

For those who are a part of the kingdom of God, prayer is a necessary tool that allows information and data to go to and from the throne of grace. Prayer allows God to download knowledge, wisdom, finances, health, body parts, healings, peace, joy, hope, and anything else that is needed in this realm to fulfill the kingdom agenda.

There are three different levels of prayer:

1. **Asking**. In this level, petition God for whatever you like.

2. **Looking**. This is intercession where you go into the spirit realm to find answers and the will of God for a people, place, or situation.

3. **Knocking**. This is when you use force to reach and get the attention of God uninvited. On this level you

can ask God to reverse things or even do things that He hasn't planned. This is what Abram was doing when he asked God to not destroy the people if he could find one righteous man.

1. **Asking**.

Ask, and it will be given to you; seek, and you will find; knock, and it will be opened to you. For everyone who asks receives, and the one who seeks finds, and to the one who knocks it will be opened. Or which one of you, if his son asks him for bread, will give him a stone? Or if he asks for a fish, will give him a serpent? If you then, who are evil, know how to give good gifts to your children, how much more will your Father who is in heaven give good things to those who ask him! (Matthew 7:7-11)

The level of asking is a level that we all start out in prayer. At this level, we aren't fully sure of the things that belong to us or that we have a right to. No one has to ask for anything that belongs to them. This level really helps us to find out who we are. In scripture, the things that are asked for are things that must be given. Therefore, things that you have access to, you shouldn't ask for. You must read your bible so that you will know what your inheritance is as a son of God.

2. **Looking**

Therefore I tell you, do not be anxious about your life, what you will eat or what you will drink, nor about your body, what you will put on. Is not life more than food, and the body more than clothing? (Matthew 6:25)

Therefore do not be anxious, saying, 'What shall we eat?' or 'What shall we drink?' or 'What shall we wear?' For the Gentiles seek after all these things, and your heavenly Father knows that you need them all. But seek first the kingdom of God and his righteousness, and all these things will be added to you. (Matthew 6:31-33)

We don't even have to ask for these things because they are already provided for us daily. As long as there is time, and within time are days, we will never have to worry about clothing, food, housing or any bare necessities.

We can stop spending so much time asking and crying for these things because they will come without our asking. I'm not suggesting that it's wrong to pray for them, but these are things that are available. Our job is to find them. Animals don't ask where they are going to sleep. They will look until they find it.

The bible tells us to seek and we will find. We must, through the power of prayer, search out the things that are provided for us. There is a divine providence available to everyone that has been blood bought by Jesus. We must pray in a manner in which we are seeking within the spirit realm for the things we need. You cannot find what is not available. There are some things that are available to all of us. Our job is to find them.

Some of us are going without what we need because we are lazy when it comes to prayer and we don't want to look for anything. There are plans and strategies available to us to solve all type of problems, but we must access them.

Ask God, in the spirit, to open up the eyes of your understanding so that you may see what you need to see.

The eyes of your understanding being enlightened; that ye may know what is the hope of his calling, and what the riches of the glory of his inheritance in the saints. And what is the exceeding greatness of his power toward us who believe, according to the working of his mighty power (Ephesians 1:18-19)

When your spiritual eyes are open, you will be able to understand the expectations of the position of Christ and His realm of power. This power, that is Christ, is the same power working in us. When you begin to see, you always see a way out, a way in, and a way through. Your vision would be according to His power. It's a perceptional change.

3. Knocking

Knock and it will be open unto you. This third level of prayer isn't reached by many people because we are not consistent in prayer.

The word "knock," is an action word which means to strike a sharp audible blow or series of blows, as on a door, or to produce by hitting or striking.

We can go to a place in prayer where we can reach heaven and cause or create a sound. This sound will cause heaven to respond to our cry and request. This is the type of prayer that doesn't end in five or so days, but it is required to get heaven to move on earth.

Prophetess Anna stayed in the sanctuary, praying and fasting until Jesus came. She and Simon prayed for many years and did not give up.

These are the type of prayers that cause revivals and that cause people to enter into deeper levels of the Spirit, with healing, and deliverances. This is the kind that is saying, "I know that you are there and I have a right to it. I can even see it. Give it to me now."

There is also a prophetic dimension of prayer which is accessible through intercession. This level of prayer tends to cause us to pray about things that are outside of time. It corrects things in the past, such as dealing with generational curses, or to give you intelligence regarding certain spirits that you may have to confront or that are after you. In this dimension of prayer, you can also move in front of time to prevent certain things from happening.

You can cancel demonic assignments, plots, and even prepare you for something that you must go through.

When I was about 12 years old, I was in prayer for my mom and my brother. I prayed for their minds, and that the peace of God would be in their hearts. I was led by the Holy Spirit to get a book entitled "How to Cope with Divorce."

At the time, I was not aware that my parents were having marital problems. As time went by, I began to see the things that the book informed me of. I was in a position to help our family deal with divorce because I was obedient to the Spirit and read the book.

My mom found my book and asked me what made me get the book. I told her that I didn't know, but God told me to read it. I then begin to share with her what I had learned.

During that time, I saw what the devil had planned, but it didn't work. His ambush was exposed. That divorce was meant to cripple me and my brother and cause us to hate our father. That would make it difficult for us to have a relationship with our Heavenly Father.

People who don't have good relationships with their natural fathers may have difficult times trusting God the Father. They are surprised at the love and the care that He has toward us. Even in discipline, Father God only chastise those He love.

I have talked about these few different types of prayer, but you need the Holy Spirit in order to pray properly.

In the same way, the Spirit helps us in our weakness. We do not know what we ought to pray for, but the Spirit himself intercedes for us through wordless groans. Romans 8:26

The Holy Spirit assists us and prays for us through wordless groans. Have you ever reached a place in prayer that you get so deep that you cease to have words? This is when the Spirit is praying for you! The Spirit communicates to God on your behalf and deal with issues you might not be strong enough to handle. Since the Spirit isn't limited by time, it can deal with things we can't currently see. We should always pray in the spirit and the natural.

What is it then? I will pray with the spirit, and I will pray with the understanding also: I will sing with the spirit, and I will sing with the understanding also. 1 Corinthians 14:15

Throughout time, the things that you will pray in the Spirit about will drop down in your heart, so that you can pray with an understanding the things that the Spirit has communicated on our behalf. I have even asked God for the interpretation.

For this reason the one who speaks in a tongue should pray that they may interpret what they say. (1 Corinthians 14:13)

3] Hearing The Voice of God

Hearing the voice of God is very important. It is a must.

My sheep hear my voice, and I know them, and they follow me. John 10:27

It is highly questionable whether you are of God if you can't hear His voice. I have met many people and taught many classes where people will get really concerned that they never hear God speak. I tend to believe that they just don't recognize His voice when they hear it.

The church has been conditioned to think that God speaks in a big, deep "James Earl Jones" type of voice. He doesn't. I have heard the audible voice of God twice and I can't explain the sound. Every part of me shook, even my skin. I knew for sure it was the voice of God.

The first time I heard God's voice audibly I was 13 years old. I was in my room, sitting on the floor, and writing songs. I heard Him say, "PREACH."

I shook so hard I thought the room was shaking too. I jumped up and ran into the middle of the street and begin to cry. I was in awe that God spoke to me and told me to preach. I went to my pastor to tell him. He said, "I know. I've been waiting on you to come to me."

Hearing the voice of God is very important, especially to those who have been called into the office of a Prophet, it's necessary.

Indeed, the Sovereign LORD never does anything until he reveals his plans to his servants the prophets. (Amos 3:7 NLT)

We must be available to hear what God has to say to the church!

Having a ready ear is making sure our own agendas and ideas don't block up our spiritual ears to hear. We could have avoided some negative events from happening to us and our family if we had only heard what God was saying. Through prophetic intercession, many plans of the enemy are exposed.

In Genesis 18, there is a conversation between Abraham and God regarding Sodom. God told Abraham that He wanted to destroy the city. He told Abraham before he did it. Abraham asked what would happen if he found some righteous people. Would God spare the city? God said, "Yes!"

God informed Abraham before He did anything because humans have dominion on earth. Spirits do not have the right to do anything on earth without the permission and cooperation of a human. Even Jesus had to come in a fleshly body in order to fulfill the agenda of God on earth.

Abraham couldn't find anybody righteous in the city. God allowed Lot and his family to be escorted out because of the relationship Abraham and God had. Abraham had mastered the "art of hearing God." We know this because Abraham followed instructions from God.

We never have to worry about disembodied spirits. They can do nothing to us in the earth realm. We outrank them here. When Jacob was wrestling with an angel, a celestial being, all night, he was successful. Outside of this realm you must use your spiritual authority, which has been delegated by Jesus Christ.

God likes to inform us before things happen. This is the pace of a prophet. Oftentimes, God will inform you before a thing happens so that you can act, prepare, or in some instances prevent a thing from happening.

Understanding this pace, you'll expect to show up first, or to even wait. God will send us to a man that isn't even home yet. Prophet Samuel showed up to Jesse's house before Saul. What you are looking for might not be there, but wait. It will come.

Now the LORD had told Samuel in his ear a day before Saul came, saying, Tomorrow about this time I will send thee a man out of the land of Benjamin, and thou shalt anoint him to be captain over my people Israel, that he may save my people out of the hand of the Philistines: for I have looked upon my people, because their cry is come unto me. I Samuel 9:15-16

Have faith in your ability to hear God correctly. God could be downloading information that could change a nation. The Prophet Samuel heard about Saul a day before he met him. People can't understand why you are saying what you're saying because you are a day before the rest.

PROPHETIC PEOPLE ARE DIFFERENT

Prophetic people are unique. I have seen some with colorful hair. They don't seem to fit in traditional settings. Some are like me, and refuse to wear suits unless they absolutely have too.

One time I had to minister at my home church and as I was walking into the church. I was stopped by another minister who told me that God wouldn't use me if I kept wearing a hair scarf. I laughed now, because as God used me to deliver a message to the church, that same minister was so touched that he apologized to me because he had spoken in error. Since that moment, I realized that in the traditional church, we train people to look anointed but these people are not always anointed.

Ye shall know them by their fruits. Do men gather grapes of thorns, or figs of thistles? We don't know you by your outward appearance but it's what is in you that we can identify if you be of the faith or not. Matthew 7:16

When we look at most of the Old Testament examples of the prophets they were very odd and peculiar people, who had odd experiences. If within the 21st century we did half of what they did, we'd be classified as lunatics and crazy deranged people.

Consider Isaiah, who stripped off all his clothes and wandered around naked (Isaiah 20).

Jeremiah, who not only hid his underwear in a rock but then went back to retrieve it after a "long time" (Jeremiah 13). Jeremiah apparently didn't mind parting with under garments, but he couldn't be separated from the cattle yoke he had fastened to his shoulders until another prophet broke it off (Jeremiah 27 and 28).

Think about Hosea, who married a prostitute and named their daughter Lo-ruhama, which means 'unloved' (Hosea 1).

Then there was Jonah, the run-away prophet who spent three days in the belly of a whale before answering God's call. When he eventually got around to preaching in Nineveh, the entire city repented. For any other preacher this would have been a joyous outcome. But Jonah was upset because of two reasons; First because he didn't want to deliver such a heavy sad judgment word; Second because he knew God was going to change his mind making it seem as if the prophecy was off or wrong. Jonah then wanted to commit suicide but knew God wouldn't allow him to so he asked God to kill him and God would not honor his request.

When looking at thee prophet Christ (Christ is the perfect example of all gifts), we can look back at these prophets and see them as foreshadowing Him—not just through the prophecies that told of His coming, but through their prophetic actions. Christ was, after all, the Word Made Flesh in the fullest and richest manner possible. And, like the prophets, Christ's behavior was considered bizarre, disruptive, unorthodox, and confusing according to social standards of the day.

I encourage prophets to make sure they cultivate a relationship with themselves. You will not fit in most social factions

At that time the kingdom of heaven will be like ten virgins who took their lamps and went out to meet the bridegroom. Five of them were foolish and five were wise. The foolish ones took their lamps but did not take any oil with them. The wise ones, however, took oil in jars along with their lamps. Matthew 25:1-4

All ten of the virgins had lamps but what made the difference was that only five of them had oil for the lamps. You may have a lamp, the ability to present a sermon, even possess oratorical finesse, but it's the oil that makes the difference. The anointing destroys the yokes. Without the anointing, you are only providing people with a description of a problem instead of a solution to be delivered. The anointing gives us access to the bridegroom, where we can receive revelation for ours and others situations.

Then he went up from there to Bethel; and as he was going up by the way, young lads came out from the city and mocked him and said to him, "Go up, you baldhead; go up, you baldhead!" When he looked behind him and saw them, he cursed them in the name of the LORD. Then two female bears came out of the woods and tore up forty-two lads of their number. And he went from there to Mount Carmel, and from there he returned to Samaria. 3 Kings 2:23-25

The Prophet Elisha had spent so much time in the prophetic that he looked different and was hidden in such a glory that some young people begin to mock him and call him baldheaded. This was to suggest that he had no spiritual covering or headship, or even back up. The prophet didn't try to explain why he was bald or what he was doing, but he called the bears from the forest to deal with those young people.

We must be careful how we deal with prophetic people. Speaking and talking against them is very

42

dangerous. It is speaking against the voice and word of God.

A prophet is one who not only speaks or delivers messages for God but is a kingdom ambassador and representative! Every prophet has the full backing of the Kingdom of Heaven, including angelic assistances and security.

Prophets need this type of security and support because of the words and information that they receive from God. The word is that important and it is very important that you can hear from God.

4] The Absolute Truth

TWO TYPES OF TRUTH

I was on a train in Washington, D.C. and was communing with God. He impressed in my spirit the importance of His Word. He said to me very clearly, "When I speak, concentrate!"

It was odd for me to hear God say that to me because I thought that I listened pretty well. I've done the things that I've been instructed to do, some made me seem pretty silly in human eyes, but I am not one to disobey the voice of God. He then gave me the scripture which added to what he said. This isn't an unfamiliar method when God is making Himself clear to us.

God never contradicts Himself. God will not speak a word that doesn't agree with the, written Word or the Logos. God does inspire spoken words, the "Rhema," but the Logos becomes the foundation to any new God ordained theological concept. God will not speak to you a unless you already know His word or have a good foundation of the Logos.

As a Chancellor of a School of Prophets, I understand why the Prophet Samuel established his school. He saw firsthand how Eli's sons mistreated, misinterpreted, and mishandled the things that were holy.

There is a certain way we must handle the Holy things. Only certain people were allowed to touch the Ark of the Covenant. You must have divine authorization!

It was the goal of the school of prophets to make sure those who were called would become well orientated with the things that were holy so that they wouldn't mistreat God's things. The goal was also to make sure the things that were spoken of God were not *lost*.

SINCE ALL this is true, we ought to pay much closer attention than ever to the truths that we have heard, lest in any way we drift past [them] and slip away. Hebrews 2:1 AMP

We must adhere to what God is speaking because God's word is absolute. His words are consistently true. This speaks volumes because there are 2 levels of truth.

1. Current truth.

This is a statement or status that is currently true but doesn't have to remain in that position permanently.

My grandfather, Bishop Robert Owens, tells a story about a preacher he once knew who would get in the pulpit and say, "I know for sure I'm living saved now." He put great emphasis on "now." I thought this was a great example on current truth, because at that moment he was sure he was doing the work of God. Whether or not or he would always do it remained to be seen.

2. Absolute truth.

This is a statement or status that is sure and is not influenced by anything outside of itself. This explains the word of God.

No matter what the outside presents, it is true within itself. When we read scripture we must read it with understanding. That it is absolute truth.

We read Isa 53:5, "...*by His stripes we are healed,*" and understand that sickness is out of line and doesn't have a right in those who are of Christ.

We must concentrate on the word of God, lest it slip away. Hebrew 2:1 describes this slipping away. It is a broken vessel or one with holes in it. We are vessels and we can be subject to cracks if we are wavering concerning God's word. Issues of life can make the word slip out your mind.

The Psalmist David declared that he would hide the word in his heart (Ps119:11). He would put the word of God in a place where it will have continuous consciousness; therefore he would not sin against God. Sin comes in when we no longer recognize what God has said as absolute truth. Isn't that what Satan said to Eve? "You shall not surely die." Sin then came in.

For if the message given through angels [the Law spoken by them to Moses] was authentic and proved sure, and every violation and disobedience received an appropriate (just and adequate) penalty. (Hebrew 2:2)

When we are living the penalty of the violation of the words of God, it is sin. We deserve whatever happens to us when we step away from the absolute word of God.

5] Divine Protection as a Prophet

YOUR PROTECTION IS THE RESPONSIBILITY OF HEAVEN

As Kingdom Ambassadors, we are constantly under attack by the demonic kingdom. The enemy will attempt to derail us daily through his many slightly cleaver tactics. It seems like you can never let your guard down. This can be very frustrating.

It is good to know that as a prophet not only do you have the responsibility of an ambassador or a divine government official, you have the support and protection of heaven. When people see you seemingly alone they don't realize that all of heaven, its hosts, and those who are assigned to you are awaiting your call.

UNDER THE PROTECTION OF THE ANGELS

This support is always prepared to be deployed to assist you in any capacity. This heavenly aid is available to those who are within the will of God, completing their divine assignment.

I'm talking about angels! Many people within the charismatic church don't touch the subject of angels and when they do its very mystical and doesn't come with much information.

The subject of angels is not well known because the canonical scripture or the authorized text does not touch the topic in terms of their ranking, position, and duties. There are more scriptures that are not in the canonical text regarding angels. Research other material.

Sadducees didn't believe in angels (Acts 23:8), like many believers today don't either. We tend to look at them as extinct creatures such as dinosaurs. As if they once were but not anymore, this certainly isn't true.

I believe this is because every reference to angels is incidental to some other topic. They are not treated in themselves. God's revelation never aims at informing us regarding the nature of angels. When they are mentioned, it is always in order to inform us further about God, what he does, and how he does it. Since details about angels are not significant for that purpose, they tend to be omitted.

The doctrine of angels holds an important place in the Word of God, it is often viewed as a difficult subject because, while there is abundant mention of angels in the Bible, the nature of this revelation is without the same kind of explicit description we often find with other subjects developed in the Bible.

Angels are created beings and not the spirits of departed or glorified human beings is brought out in Psalm 148. There the Psalmist calls on all in the celestial heavens, including the angels, to praise God. The reason given is, "For He commanded and they were created" (Ps. 148:1-5). The angels as well as the celestial heavens are declared to be created by God

There are three tiers and three rankings of angels in each tier, with equally nine orders or rankings in total. Ranking 1 as highest and 9 as lowest.

1.) Seraphim – These angels are responsible for the Throne of God. They minister to Him and His Throne. These are the ones according Isaiah 6:1-7, which cry out, "Holy Holy Holy is the Lord of Host."

They can look scary. They have two wings to cover their face, two wings to cover their feet, and they have two wings to fly. They cover their face because there can be no other image in the presence of God the King of the universe. Their feet are covered because they have no other agenda or nowhere else to go. I like to call them, "the custodians of glory." They maintain the glory of the Throne.

2.) Cherubim – These angles are guardians of the glory of God and the things that are Holy. Lucifer was a Cherub. When Adam and Eve were escorted out of the Garden of Eden there was an angel with a flaming sword guarding the garden from them so they couldn't return. (Genesis 3:24). During the Apocalypse, it will be the cherubs who will assist God (Rev 4-6).

3.) Thrones – This is the last of the first tier of angels. Not much is known about these angels. It is said that these angels act as liaisons between the lower ranking angels and God. Lower ranking angels need a certain security clearance to approach God. In angelology studies, we discovered that these angels live in the cosmos where material things take form.

For by him were all things created, that are in heaven, and that are in earth, visible and invisible, whether they be thrones, or dominions, or principalities, or powers: all things were created by him, and for him. (Colossians 1:16)

Thrones are also known as Ophanim. The word, "Ophanim" means wheel. This is what Daniel saw in Daniel 7:9.

Ezekiel 10:17 also talks about them. These angels work closely with the Cherubim. Their movements are synchronized. They move with each other in perfect precision.

4.) Dominions - Dominions provide supervision to the angels. They ensure that the commands of God are being constantly fulfilled by regulating the duties of the angels. Each is over a certain domain. Dominions can be found in Ephesians 1:21. Another name for Dominions is Lordship.

5.) Virtues - Virtues tackle strongholds on the diabolical side. I like to call them the administrators of the universe. They are known as spirits of motion and are responsible for all activities in the cosmos, such as seasons on earth and making sure they all operate in order etc. They manage movements within the heavenly bodies.

In Joshua 10:13 when Joshua needed some more time to fight in the battle, he prayed and the sun and moon stood still. He was given an extra hour. Virtues coordinated this. They couldn't just stop the earth from rotating. They had to stop the entire universe to ensure that there wasn't some type of cosmic collision in space.

6.) Powers and Authorities – Powers are mentioned in Ephesians 3:10. These angels are warring angels loyal to God and His people in the earth realm. Not only are they defenders, but they are bearers of consciousness and record keepers of history. Ephesians 6:12 also show us that the diabolical side has imitated this ranking and position as well. Powers also distribute power to individuals.

7.) Principalities and Rulers – These carry out the task given to them by dominions, and they are also responsible for groups of people. They act as blessings managers, making sure that the blessings that are allocated to us get to us. Some even suggest the idea that the arts, songs, and liberal arts are inspired by them.

8.) Archangels – The term arch means chief or first in ranking. These angels are captains, generals, and leaders among the different rankings of angels. The angel Michael is an archangel responsible for the defense ministry of heaven. Raphael is the archangel over the ministry of health.

9.) Angels – All are angels, but those without ranking are still messengers. Their responsibilities and functions differ.

Three other classifications of angels remain:

1. Elect Angels: In 1 Timothy 5:21, Paul speaks of "the elect angels." These are the holy angels who are somehow included in the elect purposes of God. These are angels who did not follow after Satan in his rebellion. There is little revealed about their election, but apparently there was a probationary period for the angelic world and these, being the elect of God, remained faithful and are confirmed in their holy state in the service of the Lord. As Chafer writes, "The fall of some angels is no more unanticipated by God than the fall of man. It may be implied, also that angels have passed a period of probation."29

2. The Living Creatures: These are angelic creatures who seem to be involved with revealing the glory of the God of Israel in His omniscience, omnipotence,

and omnipresence (Ezek. 1:5f; Rev. 4:6; 6:1). Ezekiel 10:15, 20 reveal them as cherubim. Through the four faces, they may also anticipate what God would do to bring salvation to man through His Son: (a) The face of the man suggests wisdom, compassion, intelligence and pictures Christ's humanity as the Son of man, the special focus found in the gospel of Luke; (b) the face of a lion speaks of kingly appearance and pictures Christ as King which is Matthew's emphasis; (c) the face of a bull or ox portrays a servant, the emphasis seen in Mark; and (d) the face of an eagle speaks of heavenly action and portrays the deity Christ, which is John's emphasis.

3. Watchers: "Watchers" is an Aramaic word which means, "vigilant, waking, watchful." Verse 17 may infer this is a special type of angel (if a special class is intended). It seems to describe holy angels who are constantly vigilant to serve the Lord and who watch over the rulers of the world and the affairs of men (Dan. 4:13, 17, 23). The added description, "a holy one" in verse 13 may imply there are unholy watchers, i.e., demonic forces who are watching the affairs of men and seeking to influence and destroy.

Spirits and angels are all created beings. They are not to be worshiped as we have been warned in Colossians 2:8. Angels are our helps ministers according to Hebrews 1:14. The Apostle Paul explained this in I Corinthians 13:1. *"I speak in tongues of men and of angels."* When he spoke, angels responded. He was able to deploy angelic armies.

When Jesus was on the cross, he said that if I he wanted to, he can could his Dad and at once 12 legions of angels would be deployed, He did not lose his life, he laid it down. (Matthew 26:53)

Be careful when studying angels on your own. There are many demonic teachings and theories about angels. All the studies you look into should have biblical backing before you accept the teaching.

Angels have several different responsibilities and assignments. They are equipped with supernatural strength and knowledge. I remind myself about the story when one angel killed 185,000 people in one night.

Therefore thus saith the LORD concerning the king of Assyria, He shall not come into this city, nor shoot an arrow there, nor come before it with shields, nor cast a bank against it. By the way that he came, by the same shall he return, and shall not come into this city, saith the LORD. For I will defend this city to save it for mine own sake, and for my servant David's sake. Then the angel of the LORD went forth, and smote in the camp of the Assyrians a hundred and fourscore and five thousand: and when they arose early in the morning, behold, they were all dead corpses. Isaiah 37:33-36

Since I listed some of the demonic princes I would be remised if I did not mention the 7 Archangels of the Divine. Note this list is mentioned in the book of

Enoch which is considered an apocrypha text and not found in the canonical bible.

•   **Michael** in the Hebrew language means "Who is like God?" or "Who is equal to God?" St. Michael has been depicted from earliest Christian times as a commander, who holds in his right hand a spear with which he attacks Lucifer/Satan, and in his left hand a green palm branch. At the top of the spear there is a linen ribbon with a red cross. The Archangel Michael is especially considered to be the Guardian of the Orthodox Faith and a fighter against heresies.

•   **Gabriel** means "God is my strength" or "Might of God." He is the herald of the mysteries of God, especially the Incarnation of God and all other mysteries related to it. He is depicted as follows: In his right hand, he holds a lantern with a lighted taper inside, and in his left hand, a mirror of green jasper. The mirror signifies the wisdom of God as a hidden mystery.

•   **Raphael** means "It is God who heals" or "God Heals" (Tobit 3:17, 12:15). Raphael is depicted leading Tobit (who is carrying a fish caught in the Tigris) with his right hand, and holding a physician's alabaster jar in his left hand.

•   **Uriel** means "God is my light," or "Light of God" (II Esdras 4:1, 5:20). He is depicted holding a sword against the Persians in his right hand, and a flame in his left.

• **Sealtiel** means "Intercessor of God." He is depicted with his face and eyes lowered, holding his hands on his bosom in prayer.

• **Jegudiel** means "Glorifier of God." He is depicted bearing a golden wreath in his right hand and a triple-thonged whip in his left hand.

• **Barachiel** means "Blessed by God." He is depicted holding a white rose in his hand against his breast.

• **Jerahmeel** means "God's exaltation." He is venerated as an inspirer and awakener of exalted thoughts that raise a person toward God (II Esdras 4:36). As an eighth, he is sometimes included as archangel.

God has you covered. As a vessel of God, you don't have to worry about your protection. There is assistance outside of this world waiting for the voice of His call. When people see you they may not realize that you come with the backing of God Himself, the Creator of the Universe.

There was recorded a time when the prophet Elisha had to pray for one of his mentees, that his eyes be open so that he can see that there was more for them then that were against them.

Then Elisha prayed and said, "O LORD, I pray, open his eyes that he may see." And the LORD opened the servant's eyes and he saw; and behold, the mountain was full of horses and chariots of fire all around Elisha. 2 Kings 6:17

There is no need to be afraid. You have back up.

Here is more biblical proof.

He permitted no man to oppress them, And He reproved kings for their sakes, saying, "Do not touch My anointed ones, And do My prophets no harm." 1 Chronicles 16:21-22

"My God sent His angel and shut the lions' mouths and they have not harmed me, inasmuch as I was found innocent before Him; and also toward you, O king, I have committed no crime. Daniel 6:22

But the Lord is faithful, and He will strengthen and protect you from the evil one. (2 Thessalonians 3:3)

6] Conquering Loneliness

THE LONELY PROPHET

Every prophet must overcome loneliness. I consider loneliness a crown which represents that you are mature enough to lead and to provide oversight. Loneliness is deeper than not having people around you or having fellowship. You can experience it even in a room full of people, in a relationship, or around loved ones.

Some would suggest that it is a spirit that is not of God, mainly because we've been taught that God will never leave us alone nor abandon us. But this announcement would only be given if it was expected that a time would come when you would feel or meet this spirit of loneliness.

Loneliness is the time and space designated by God for development and redefinition of self.

During my greatest times of loneliness, God was requiring my paradigm to shift to another level that my current environment had not reached. This is scary because this type of shift requires everything to change at once. Without notice, the things which did look like home or were familiar, become strange.

This is because God is leading you to a higher place, a new place. You'll have to leave good people, friends and family, not because they were bad or negative, but because God has better plans for you.

The enemy of better is good. God knows that the level He needs for us to reach will destroy those who weren't made for the new level.

Prophet Jeremiah is one of the most noted prophets in the Old Testament. Preachers love to talk about the fact that he was born a prophet before the foundations of the world. Even before he was placed into his mother's womb, he was a powerful man of God. He was called as a young man to correct a corrupt system that existed before he showed up in the earth.

He had a huge assignment on his shoulders and what made it even heavier is that God required that he remained alone, unmarried, and no children! (Jer. 16:1-5).

He wasn't allowed to participate in social events, not even funerals. He preached a messaged that no one liked. His messages were never inspirational or catchy so that he could get preaching engagements or so that people would like him. People laughed and talked about him constantly.

"Alas, my mother, that you gave me birth, a man with

whom the whole land strives and contends! I have neither lent nor borrowed, yet everyone curses me! . . ."

"I am ridiculed all day long; everyone mocks me. Whenever I speak, I cry out proclaiming violence and destruction. So the word of the LORD has brought me insult and reproach all day long" (Jer. 15:10 and 20:7-8).

God used Jeremiah's life as a prophetic demonstration to show the people of God that they will be isolated from the world if they didn't comply to the voice of the Lord from His prophet.

Although you read about the complaints that Jeremiah had about his loneliness, it was the loneliness that gave him the authority he needed to fulfill his assignment. It was this crown that people recognized that he was truly a man of God and a voice to the nation. Had Jeremiah not overcome this he would have never been able to say "I know the thoughts that I have toward you, they are good and to give you an expected in..." (Jer 29:11)

This was said right after another prophet had a "good" prophecy that relief was coming and that the bondage the people were suffering was going to end. Conquering loneliness enabled him to stand against the popular word of freedom to say, "Not yet... but trust me, God has a plan and it's going to be good and you will be coming out, but just not today."

During his times alone Jeremiah discovered two things. He discovered who God is and who he was, in relationship to who God is.

Even the spiritual ranking of Prophet Jeremiah had an impact on his separation.

There is a distinct difference between ranking and gifting. Although the gifting may outrank other gifts there still is ranking within the gifts. This is required to maintain structure.

I never sat in the company of revelers, never made merry with them; I sat alone because your hand was on me and you had filled me with indignation. Jeremiah 15:17

The scripture says, *"he sat alone because the hand of the Lord was upon him."*

God had to separate him, even within the office, because of his ranking. He sat too high to be common with those he outranked. He wasn't better but familiarity can birth out disrespect and that cannot and will not be tolerated with the Kingdom. This is spiritual protocol.

We must be careful not to sit with those who are immature or who we outrank unless we are teaching them. We shouldn't share everything with them, because in times of reproof, it will back fire on you. They'll think that because you are a friend, you have no spiritual authority.

We must learn to talk with the Holy Spirit in prayer about everything. He is not shocked by our concerns. He can handle our concerns about relationship, sex, finances, occupations, ministry, health and fitness, and anything else.

You can determine the ranking by the level and amount of access to God that an individual has. The higher the ranking, the more intimate the interactions between God and the individual will be. The classification level of information is also determined by the ranking. God will not talk to you about governments unless that is the level you are on. If He is discussing with you about your neighborhood, that is the level you are currently on.

LONELY IN A CROWDED ROOM

Some would call me a socialite. I'm not sure if I was very popular but I made sure I was always invited to the events that mattered. Whether it was a political event, a church service, party, a club opening, I liked to be in the house.

One night, around four o'clock in the morning, I had been to several parties. Lots of cocktails were in my system. The music was pounding in my ears and everyone seemed to be happy to see me. As I greeted and hugged those in the room, it hit me. In a room full of people, I felt a loneliness so heavy I had to take another shot so that I wouldn't cry.

I went to the car while the folks I was with continued to party. I tried to count in my head the number of people I could count on if I had to. The more I thought about this, the worse I felt. I knew a lot of people but hardly anyone knew the real me.

People could count on me to do what they needed, but in my time of need, I didn't have many people I could go to. The Holy Spirit told me, "Son, you must master the spirit of loneliness, or greatness will kill you."

These words, although they weren't necessarily "happy" words, soothed my soul because I knew what I was up against and that I could master this spirit.

A LONELY POSITION

And Miriam and Aaron spake against Moses because of the Ethiopian woman whom he had married: for he had married an Ethiopian woman. And they said, Hath the LORD indeed spoken only by Moses? hath he not spoken also by us? And the LORD heard it. (Now the man Moses was very meek, above all the men which were upon the face of the earth.) And the LORD spake suddenly unto Moses, and unto Aaron, and unto Miriam, Come out ye three unto the tabernacle of the congregation. And they three came out. And the LORD came down in the pillar of the cloud, and stood in the door of the tabernacle, and called Aaron and Miriam: and they both came forth. And he said, Hear now my words: If there be a prophet among you, I the LORD will make myself known unto him in a vision, and will speak unto him in a dream. My servant Moses is not so, who is faithful in all mine house. With him will I speak mouth to mouth, even apparently, and not in dark speeches; and the similitude of the LORD shall he behold: wherefore then were ye not afraid to speak against my servant Moses? And the anger of the LORD was kindled against them; and he departed. And the cloud departed from off the tabernacle; and, behold, Miriam became leprous, white as snow: and Aaron looked upon Miriam, and, behold, she was leprous. And Aaron said unto Moses, Alas, my lord, I beseech thee, lay not the sin upon us, wherein we have done foolishly, and wherein we have sinned. (Numbers 12:1-11)

This was a discussion among brothers and sisters in the natural, but also in the spirit realm. It started over who

Moses decided to marry. This seemed like a normal conversation amongst siblings.

The problem was that Moses wasn't only their brother, but also one of God's generals. Miriam and Aaron were both prophetic people as well, but the discussion regarding whether or not God was pleased with his decision to marry his wife was a spiritual matter and they moved outside of rights and authority by having the conversation.

God then called for a meeting amongst the three. Because Moses was a humble man, he still never said anything. The higher your ranking, the more humble you are required to be.

My mom's definition of humble is "to have power that is controlled." Moses had the power to react to their conversation but he allowed God to handle it. Humbleness is understanding that just because you can doesn't mean that you will.

God explained who Moses was to Him and his importance. He told them that the way that He spoke to prophets was through dreams, visions, and scenarios that need to be decoded. He spoke to others through messages from angels and other messengers, but Moses was different because of his ranking. He spoke to Moses directly, face to face. Moses was God's main contact in the earth. Moses had the capacity and depth that could handle a direct word from God.

Moses never confronted them about their conversation. God intervened because they were disrespecting the office, position, and ranking that God placed their brother in. Both Miriam and Aaron were older than Moses, but he still outranked them.

God asked Miriam and Aaron why they thought it was okay for them to discuss His ambassador. Moses was God's man and God would handle him directly.

Please be careful how you speak about someone who is of God. I have suffered many things because I spoke on things that I did not understand.

Miriam was struck with leprosy due to her reckless conversation and her not understanding the position he held.

This does not give leaders the right to treat people poorly or be disrespectful, but we must allow God to handle them. Your submission to them has nothing to do with them but to God through them. Spiritual protocol is not natural. Our obedience to leadership has nothing to do with a person but the office and rank that God has given them.

To remain in divine order, respect the office even when the person's personality isn't reflective of the office. I know some people who are very difficult to deal with because of their personality but I will never break protocol or disrespect them or call them out. I won't uncover them because if I do, I would have to deal with God, just as they will have to if they are out of order.

When God speaks to me, whether it is a personal word or for someone else in the body of Christ, I am greatly impacted. Sometimes, He will speak one word and it blows my mind to such a level that it takes me a few days to come down from the impact of the word. It rattles my brain and challenges my intellect.

God said to me one day, "I got you."

That one word still affects me. When God speaks it's the same in every level and dimension. He is the same today, yesterday, and forever more. He is in all three of those times now.

When God said, "I got you," it didn't only mean then at that time but at all times in all dimensions at any level. I can be fully secured that I am in the hands and arms of God, Himself.

The ranking of God has nothing to do with age. The Apostle Paul told Timothy that he shouldn't let anyone despise him because of his youth. Timothy may have been younger, but he outranked those under him.

God will not communicate with everyone. Since He communes with you, not everyone can commune with you. You are a special apostolic, prophetic, evangelistic, pastoral, teaching agent for heaven. This limits your connection to others because we are on call at all times.

God needs to be able to contact us at all times. You can't go everywhere. You are the property of heaven and they can't risk your demise. Your spirit can't be in fellowship with other spirits that may penetrate your spirit. The kingdom cannot risk that type of security breach.

You will be alone sometimes and go through seasons where you feel all alone but know that you're never alone. Jesus will never leave us nor forsake us. We have the Holy Spirit dwelling inside us and a host of angels encamped all around us!

God will also send in others who can handle the same yoke that you carry. You'll have some covenant relationships as God sends people. For all others, ask the Holy Spirit what their role and position is in your life. You must handle and master being alone or you'll never enter the higher levels of the spirit.

7] Overcoming Carnality

THE CARNAL MIND CANNOT SUBMIT

To be carnally minded is death; but to be spiritually minded is life and peace. Romans 8:6

The spirit of loneliness comes to make you deal with the spirit of carnality.

Because I came from a "church" family, I have heard the word "carnality" throughout my life. However, I wasn't fully sure of the meaning of it. I almost thought it was to think normal and not like an unsaved person. There was some truth in that but it's much deeper.

Because the carnal mind is enmity against God: for it is not subject to the law of God, neither indeed can be. Romans 8:7

A carnal mind hates God and especially hates the submission to God and His law. The carnal mind not only refuses to submit, but wouldn't even if he could.

This chief spirit births out other sons such as disobedience, rebellion, and pride. It doesn't have the capacity to obtain the will, laws, and agenda of God. The carnal mind is too shallow to hold the idea of God or His ideas.

And I, brethren, could not speak unto you as unto spiritual, but as unto carnal, even as unto babes in Christ. I have fed you with milk, and not with meat: for hitherto ye were not able to bear it, neither yet now are ye able. For ye are yet carnal: for whereas there is among you envying, and strife, and divisions, are ye not carnal, and walk as men? For while one saith, I am of Paul; and another, I am of Apollos; are ye not carnal? Who then is Paul, and who is Apollos, but ministers by whom ye believed, even as the Lord gave to every man? I have planted, Apollos watered; but God gave the increase. So then neither is he that planteth any thing, neither he that watereth; but God that giveth the increase. I Corinthians 3:1-7

The Apostle Paul wanted to give his readers meat but could not because they weren't mature enough. You must have teeth in order to eat meat. There is a level of maturity that is required in order for you to be able to handle it. A carnal mind then also is spiritually immature. The signs of this mindset are listed as:

1.) Envy
2.) Strife
3.) Divisions

These three are sons of carnality. In the passage above, Paul wants us to accept that one person plants and another waters. The "thing" is bigger than you alone and you can only do your part. You can't do it all. You can't have the whole plan. God reveals things in part. It doesn't matter who has the other part.

The carnal mind wants credit for a move of God. No matter what part you play, whether it is watering or sowing, God is the one who brings the increase. We don't cause increase we are only to properly manage it.

"It varies with different personalities. Some will keep quiet. They have not yet attained freedom from natural shyness and fear. They may sit next to those talkative believers and criticize them in heart, but their silence does not make them any less soulish. Because they are not rooted in God and have not therefore learned how to be hidden in Him, carnal people long to be seen. They experience unspeakable joy whenever recognized and respected. Because the carnal are greatly talented - active in thought, rich in emotion - they readily arouse people's interest and stir the latter's hearts. Consequently, soulish Christians usually possess magnetic personalities. They can quickly win the acclamation of the common people. Yet the fact remains that they actually are lacking in spiritual power. They do not contain the living flow of the power of the Holy Spirit." Watchman Nee

Many apostles and prophets of today are concerned about the spirit of entertainment that has crept into the churches. It is a result of this same spirit. We are so impressed by talents, that we are using talents to identify people. That is not what shows whether someone is anointed or not. The bible tells us that we should know them by their fruit, not talent.

Ye shall know them by their fruits. Do men gather grapes of thorns, or figs of thistles? Matthew 7:16

There are devils that can sing and give us goosebumps! There are great orators who want nothing to do with God. Because we are carnal, we can't recognize that we are only being entertained and not edified.

We must check why we want to do ministry. Why do you want to prophesy or preach? Is it because you want people to know you "got it" or that you can? Is it because you want to prove you're delivered or not like you used to be? Do you want people to recognize you? Are you upset when you are overlooked or not recognized? If folks don't use your title are you offended? Do you always have to be right? Are you concerned about your reputation?

These are the questions we must deal with to determine if we are in a carnal mindset. If today you can say yes to any, you are battling with the carnal mind.

By all means, be honest with God so that you can come into the place that God has for you. It requires you to come out of the carnal mindset.

These desires are completely normal. We all like to be acknowledged and accepted for our gifts and talents, but God requires us to crucify our flesh. You are dead to yourself, that He may be alive in you!

For we know that the law is spiritual: but I am carnal, sold under sin. For that which I do I allow not: for what I would, that do I not; but what I hate, that do I. If then I do that which I would not, I consent unto the law that it is good. Now then it is no more I that do it, but sin that dwelleth in me. For I know that in me (that is, in my flesh,) dwelleth no good thing: for to will is present with me; but how to perform that which is good I find not. For the good that I would I do not: but the evil which I would not, that I do. Now if I do that I would not, it is no more I that do it, but sin that dwelleth in me. I find then a law, that, when I would do good, evil is present with me. For I delight in the law of God after the inward man: But I see another law in my members, warring against the law of my mind, and bringing me into captivity to the law of sin which is in my members. Romans 7:14-23

The carnal mind and the spiritual mind abide in two different set of laws. Therefore, we expect and get different results from both. You overcome carnality when you expose its intent and when you make a decision not to submit to it but rather under the hand of God. When we submit to God, we die to self (Galatians 2:20). We submit to God's will and not our own (John 6:38). Submission to God gives us freedom to please Him.

We must always be aware of the devil, his tactics, and his kingdom, by always resisting him. (1 Peter 5:8-9). He then will flee from us. Repentance also rids us of this mindset and we ultimately strive to get closer and closer to God.

8] The CHURCH

Ephesians 4:11 And he gave some, apostles; and some, prophets; and some, evangelists; and some, pastors and teachers; 12For the perfecting of the saints, for the work of the ministry, for the edifying of the body of Christ:

1 Corinthians 12:28 And God has placed in the church first of all apostles, second prophets, third teachers, then miracles, then gifts of healing, of helping, of guidance, and of different kinds of tongues.

We hear many teachers and preachers speak about the role of the prophetic but for some odd reason we've skipped over the placement of the prophet within the church. There's a new school of thought that suggest that "prophets" are evangelist or itinerary ministers. Every prophet needs to be placed and attached to a church or body of believers. Reference 1 Cor. 12:28 God has placed in the CHURCH prophets.

When we look at the first person who was ever called a prophet in the bible in I Samuel 9:9 was the Prophet Samuel. Although we know he was not the first prophet but in terms of title and official position in the church he was. Samuel did things outside of the church but his first prophetic ministry was to the church. He had to speak to Eli the high priest regarding the state of the church. So in order for God to attempt to fix the church, He had to introduce a prophetic voice. Most people call prophets judgmental but they are designed to see and recognize foundational flaws and mistakes in the church. The prophet is like the quality control department of the body.

The prophet as the other five gifts were gift sent for the perfecting of the saints. You can't be perfect with flaws, spots, and wrinkles. The prophetic office will identify flaws along with the apostle who they are to walk with. These two gifts act as the foundation of the church of Jesus Christ.

Unfortunately, the current format of the church is incorrect and the position of the prophet and the apostle was removed from the church leadership.

They placed pastors over the church when we see clearly it says:
1st Apostles
2nd Prophets
3rd Teachers/Pastors

The aforementioned gifts/offices are listed in order of ranking. A pastor cannot cover or provide an oversight to a prophet. Reason being is because the prophet out ranks a pastor. A prophet needs an apostle.

So in the current set up of the church there is no place for the prophet or apostle, but your gift will make room for you. Notices the word "make" room, which means that when the gift shows up and if there is no place for it, the gift will readjust the entire leadership structure and some will call this "disorder".

Many prophets are not rogue or rebellious but displaced because they are looking for their place in the church. It is the displaced prophet that fall victim to all type of sorcery, witchcraft, clairvoyance, psychics, and becoming mediums.

The church is the educational system of heaven and the spirit realm, we are to be developed and educated as prophets in the church. There are rules and legalities in the spiritual realm. There's a code of conduct and etiquette. Not knowing this can put you at risk of being hurt severely.

Matthew Fox wrote in his book Creation Spirituality Liberating Gifts for the Peoples of the Earth; "the spirit realm that includes duality but goes beyond time and space, good and evil, is not to be understood properly based solely upon a dualistic perspective. All wholes manifest a synergetic effect wherein the whole is greater than the sum of its parts. The tensile strength of steel is far greater than the sum of the tensile strength of the
individual minerals and metals used to create steel. God is not One. God is whole, more than one, but less than two. And in between one and two lies infinity. God is neither alone nor all one. We are not alone. Things matter."

Prophets we must fold into the wholeness of the body of Christ. We must be part and our presence is needed to bring the body into a place of perfection.

Operating in the prophetic office in a local assembly

1 Cor 14:32 (New Living Translation)
Remember that people who prophesy are in control of their spirit and can take turns.

Do not attempt to prophesy if you have not been given a platform or a space to prophesy. I recall the feeling that I was going to explode if I didn't get out what I heard God saying and I remember hearing the spirit then tell me if they don't make room for my word DO NOT release it. You can control your spiritual gifting, it is yours.

Have you ever noticed that children usually say anything that is on their mind rather it's appropriate or not? Same thing happens with immature prophets. They can't hold a word. They lack the capacity required to wait for timing and opportunity. It denotes zealousness without knowledge.

A mature prophet among a body of believers understands that their role is far more than prophesying, preaching, or teaching. They understand that they represent the word of God amongst the body. They will help with the development of the people, namely the leaders. They most likely will head several different departments and axillaries. They will certainly act as a support and adviser to the house leadership. They will actively pray for the apostle of the assembly. Prophetic intercession is necessary and mandated.

A mature prophet understands they must multi task, they must build and protect at the same time (Nehemiah 4:16-20). Most modern day apostle will disagree with this next school of thought that I am suggesting but the prophet holds the apostle accountable to the assignment/vision given to the body by God. They keep them on track and within the right next steps for the assembly.

Keeping in mind that the prophetic office is a heavy gift and comes with a great authority, one must always be mindful that they are using their gift wisely and that they are edifying the body with their efforts. All those who come in contact with a prophet of God should be the better or at least have the opportunity to be better.

Please leave all issues of rebuke or reproof to skilled seasoned prophets and apostles. The last thing you want to do is have someone offended by your attempt to fulfill your prophetic assignment. An offended soul cannot receive from God.

Luke 7:23 (KJV) And blessed is he, whosoever shall not be offended in me.

Our goal should never be to harm or offend the body. I have seen and hear prophets enjoy saying things that would bring harm to the body and to the people they speak it too. Even in rebuking, the goal is to save the person not destroy them.

Luke 17:1 (KJV) Then said he unto the disciples, It is impossible but that offences will come: but woe unto him, through whom they come!
So then there must be a way to deliver a word or strive to correct someone without offending them. Find out how by praying in the spirit until a strategy is downloaded into your spirit. I am reminded about the story (2 Samuel 12) of when the Prophet Nathan had to rebuke Kind David. He did it with such class and made it smooth enough and plain enough for Kind David to receive and not be offended.

I am certainly sure the story would have gone another way had the Prophet Nathan not handled King David in a certain manner. It could have even cost Prophet Nathan's life. It is very important to know how to deliver the message from the Lord. This is why I promote prophetic mentorship among young prophets. (Note the youthfulness of a prophet has nothing to do with age, but rather maturity in the prophetic)

You will learn from a good prophetic mentor that there is a way the message has to be handled and delivered so that people can receive it. No matter what you see you still must deliver it appropriately.

Now since the prophetic gift is a governmental gift and a foundational gift, the prophet in you will desire to bring order to places within the administration of the church or ministry. A prophet should work close with the leaders of the church even if he or she is not the senior pastor. The prophetic insight will position the ministry correctly and keep it trending and cutting edge. The prophetic will identify the direction of the church, but note only the leader is able to take the church in that direction.

As a prophetic leader in a church we are not to fight and argue with leadership. We must learn a lesson from one of our prophetic fathers Moses. Notice when Pharaoh did not receive the prophetic word from Moses that the kingdom's economy was going to have to charge drastically. He informed him that God needed him to release all his free labor; an entire workforce. Not giving him any information or alternatives on how to replace what God has now deemed illegal. I am sure Pharaoh was empathic to the cause in terms of the people rights and human rights but he was use to the way things were. The bible even tells us that God hardened the heart of this leader. So Moses had to continue to go back to God to ask from another way to present his message.

If your message isn't received, you don't cry and have a tantrum! Go back to God and ask for another strategy to convey the message! As the prophet you are responsible for leading people towards God. We are not a GPS that only speaks the direction with no attachment or interest in the persons we are giving directions to.

Revelations are the result of a prophetic gift deciding not to give up on a word from God regarding his people! When we speak on people like Martin Luther King Jr. he certainly was a prophet likened to Moses. He did not abandon the message because people did not have the capacity to receive it. He continued to preach/prophesy and build the hearts of the people to receive.

Sometimes this may take years. You won't be able to use human or conventional measurements to track the success of a message that maybe rejected upon its first release. But notice that God is in the middle of this all. He has in his hand the heart of the king and even the pastor of a local assembly. Trust God to provide whatever is needed to fulfill the assignment He has given you.

The tension you may feel maybe from God using resistant training to build your spiritual muscles. To make you strong for other assignments along the way, making sure you can handle a no or I don't believe you! As a prophet you cannot be hypersensitive naturally. Most prophetic people strive not to fall victim to depression and other mental issues, because it is easy to fall into those mental states for prophets.

Throughout the entire bible when we look at the prophets and their dealings with the people at some point became depressed, discouraged, anxious, suicidal, and even afraid. Some didn't even want to do anything else for God because of the weight of the responsibility.

I recommend these tips while in the local assembly:

Submit to the leadership of the house – Find out who all the leaders are. Make sure you understand their roles. Develop a relationship with them. Be accountable to the leadership of the house. Do NOT take on ministry assignments outside of the ministry without discussing it with the pastor or senior. Follow all procedures and policies.

Attend Church Services Regularly –You must be present with the body you are called to. Do not take assignments on the days and times of your regularly scheduled services.

Participate – The worst thing you can do as a prophetic gift is to be among a body of believers and not participate in the many activities. Offer your help and expertise! Always be found helping.

Learn the history of the ministry – Understanding the history of the ministry will give you a lot of clarity on the current position of the church. Investigate, even spiritually. Pray and ask God about things in the ministry and why things are the way they are.

Learn the culture – Every ministry has its own way of doing things. There is a set of unspoken rules you must know! Learn them.

Be sincere – Be totally authentic. Do not fake it until you make it. Actually care for the people. Your love for God and his people has to be sincere. People can tell if you don't really like them. So even with difficult people learn to love them from the God position. Let you love for God be enough to love everyone!

 Remember they're watching you – since you proclaimed your prophetic gift openly people will watch your every step. Please be an ambassador of the kingdom. Represent the kingdom of God well.

9] Prophetic Metron and Scope of Rule

Metron is a Greek word meaning: (3358) metron (met'-ron); an apparently primary word; a measure ("metre"), literally or figuratively; by implication a limited portion (degree).

The scope of rule answers these questions. In fact, scope rules tell us if an entity (i.e., variable, parameter and function) is "visible" or accessible at certain places. Thus, places where an entity can be accessed or visible is referred to the scope of that entity.

Metron comes from the scripture: "But we will not boast of things without our measure, but according to the measure (3358) of the rule which God hath distributed to us, a measure to reach even unto you." (2 Cor 10:13 KJV)

Each person and every gift has a portioned measure of authority and influence. This portion has been allocated by God Himself to provide everything we need in order to fulfill our divine mandate. Our metron doesn't only speak of our authority but it also speaks to its limits and its boundaries. It is a very dangerous thing to go outside of these boundaries and it can cause lots of havoc injury.

2 Corinthians 10:12-18 New International Version (NIV)

12 We do not dare to classify or compare ourselves with some who commend themselves. When they measure themselves by themselves and compare themselves with themselves, they are not wise. 13 We, however, will not boast beyond proper limits, but will confine our boasting to the sphere of service God himself has assigned to us, a sphere that also includes you. 14 We are not going too far in our boasting, as would be the case if we had not come to you, for we did get as far as you with the gospel of Christ. 15 Neither do we go beyond our limits by boasting of work done by others. Our hope is that, as your faith continues to grow, our sphere of activity among you will greatly expand, 16 so that we can preach the gospel in the regions beyond you. For we do not want to boast about work already done in someone else's territory. 17 But, "Let the one who boasts boast in the Lord."[a] 18 For it is not the one who commends himself who is approved, but the one whom the Lord commends

The apostle Paul exposes to the church at Corinth that there is a measurement but the measurement is different for each of us. He explained that it is unwise to measure yourself with someone else's accomplishments or assignment. He made it aware that it is unwise to compare.

The ministry identity, style, formula, function, and tactics will all be different. We operate differently but all by the same spirit. Each of us represents a facet of God's authority and His image in the earth realm.

Metron and Scope of Rule:

Rule 1 – The scope of an entity (Apostle, Prophet, Evangelist, Pastor, Teacher) is the office, system, program, or function in which it is declared. There is a direct consequence of Rule 1. Since an entity declared in a function has a scope of that function, this entity cannot be seen from outside of the function. As stated before a person must operate within their function only. It is important that you make your calling and election sure! If one operates or attempts to operate outside of their declared entity they will go unseen, un-impactful, un-effective, and unsuccessful. One's scope of rule is their place of exists!

The declaration to any of the offices must be made by God and is declared in eternity before we were in our mother's womb. A prophet isn't made nor ordained of men. A prophet can be confirmed of men but this is a divine call from the bed chamber of God. There are and will be many prophets that will be born and will never be known in the public eye for their abilities to minister the word of God or even known for their prophecy. This doesn't make them any less a prophet; it only shows that their metron and scope of rule is different than another's.

Rule 2 – A global entity (Apostle, Prophet, Evangelist, Pastor, Teacher) is visible and recognizable to all contained functions, including the function in which that entity is declared. These are those who have global reach and revelation beyond the one office or function; people like Bishop Corletta J. Vaughn, the Late Archbishop Benson Idahosa, Dr. Cindy Trimm, David Yonggi Cho, Archbishop Nicholas Duncan Williams, Bishop Bill Hamon, the Late Great Right Rev. Robert N. Owens, and many more! Thus, the first (declared entity and global entity) two produce different results even though their actual mission may be same in terms of overall objective! To remove negative side effect with these gifts; if it is possible, avoid using global variables in internal functions. These people need to either be at the helm of a ministry or have freedom to function externally.

Rule 3 – Authenticity of an entity. An entity declared in the scope of another entity is always a different entity even if their names are same. No matter where your entity is declared your metron and rule is always personally fitted to you individually. So even if the office or the function is the same; the scope of rule is different. All prophets are not the same!

Rule 4 – A delegated entity is when one has been extended another's scoop of rule. All that is within that rule is then recognizes and accommodates the extended.

How do you discover your scope and rule?

Pray – ask God in prayer, what am I born to do?

Recognize – be clear on your assignments. Your particular assignments will denote your metron and scope of rule. If you have a global rule God will deal with you on international issues. Note He'll also provide the connections, provision, and access deemed necessary to fulfill the given assignments.

Test your reach – I think about the story when Apostle Peter jumped out of the boat and began to walk on water like Jesus. Apostle Peter learned a viable lesson. First; just because Jesus had rule over the elements didn't mean he did. Although he was known as one of Jesus' best friends they did everything together but at this moment he discovered Christ was a different entity than he. Second; Apostle Peter discovered that while he was focusing on the one who did have rule over the elements his scope of rule increased to match the one he was focusing on. In his discovery of these he was able to do many great things because he realized his scope of rule and metron was delegated and that it had to be given to him and if he focused on Christ the metron of the Messiah would be extended.

Conclusion:

I want to say thank you so much for reading this book. These are lessons that I've learned that has allowed me to keep up with the prophetic pace of the spirit realm. Yes, there is more to come, and I will go deeper but I didn't want to scare you by giving too much too fast. Too much light to soon can be blinding and dangerous.

It's my prayer that the things shared in this compact lesson book will bring you up to speed. Enlighten the eyes of your understanding, while inspiring you to continue to push into God at levels not common to most.

Uncommon places require intentional efforts to reach, your cooperation in reading this is a sign that you want to go deeper.

I am praying for you!

@ProphetCedric
www.prophetcedric.com

NOTES

NOTES

Made in the USA
Lexington, KY
12 February 2019